Sell It!

A Workbook for Selling on Social Media

by Jennifer Wallner

HOW TO USE THIS BOOK:

If you use Facebook, Instagram, Snapchat, Periscope,
etc. to sell merchandise once a week or more, this book is for you.
This workbook will help you keep track of the inventory you are showing.

Photo Cover by PlaceIt!

ISBN: 9781653732463

Date: ______________________

Theme: ____

Item Number	Item Name/Product & Description	Quantity in Stock	Price	Discount/ Sale Price

Date: ____________________

Theme: ____

Item Number	Item Name/Product & Description	Quantity in Stock	Price	Discount/ Sale Price

Date: ______________________________

Theme: ____

Item Number	Item Name/Product & Description	Quantity in Stock	Price	Discount/ Sale Price

Date: ______________________

Theme: ____

Item Number	Item Name/Product & Description	Quantity in Stock	Price	Discount/ Sale Price

Date: ____________________

Theme: ____

Item Number	Item Name/Product & Description	Quantity in Stock	Price	Discount/ Sale Price

Date: ______________________

Theme: ____

Item Number	Item Name/Product & Description	Quantity in Stock	Price	Discount/ Sale Price

Date: ______________________________

Theme: ____

Item Number	Item Name/Product & Description	Quantity in Stock	Price	Discount/ Sale Price

Date: ____________________________

Theme: ____

Item Number	Item Name/Product & Description	Quantity in Stock	Price	Discount/ Sale Price

Date: ______________________

Theme: ____

Item Number	Item Name/Product & Description	Quantity in Stock	Price	Discount/ Sale Price

Date: ____________________

Theme: ____

Item Number	Item Name/Product & Description	Quantity in Stock	Price	Discount/ Sale Price

Date: ______________________

Theme: ____

Item Number	Item Name/Product & Description	Quantity in Stock	Price	Discount/ Sale Price

Date: ______________________

Theme: ____

Item Number	Item Name/Product & Description	Quantity in Stock	Price	Discount/ Sale Price

Date: ____________________

Theme: ______________________________________

Item Number	Item Name/Product & Description	Quantity in Stock	Price	Discount/ Sale Price

Date: ______________________

Theme: ____

Item Number	Item Name/Product & Description	Quantity in Stock	Price	Discount/ Sale Price

Date: ______________________

Theme: ____

Item Number	Item Name/Product & Description	Quantity in Stock	Price	Discount/ Sale Price

Date: ______________________________

Theme: ____

Item Number	Item Name/Product & Description	Quantity in Stock	Price	Discount/ Sale Price

Date: ____________________

Theme: ______________________________

Item Number	Item Name/Product & Description	Quantity in Stock	Price	Discount/ Sale Price

Date: ______________________________

Theme: ____

Item Number	Item Name/Product & Description	Quantity in Stock	Price	Discount/ Sale Price

Date: ______________________

Theme: ____

Item Number	Item Name/Product & Description	Quantity in Stock	Price	Discount/ Sale Price

Date: ______________________

Theme: ____

Item Number	Item Name/Product & Description	Quantity in Stock	Price	Discount/ Sale Price

Date: ______________________

Theme: ____

Item Number	Item Name/Product & Description	Quantity in Stock	Price	Discount/ Sale Price

Date: ______________________________

Theme: ____

Item Number	Item Name/Product & Description	Quantity in Stock	Price	Discount/ Sale Price

Date: ____________________

Theme: ____

Item Number	Item Name/Product & Description	Quantity in Stock	Price	Discount/ Sale Price

Date: ______________________

Theme: ____

Item Number	Item Name/Product & Description	Quantity in Stock	Price	Discount/ Sale Price

Date: ______________________

Theme: ____

Item Number	Item Name/Product & Description	Quantity in Stock	Price	Discount/ Sale Price

Date: ____________________

Theme: ____

Item Number	Item Name/Product & Description	Quantity in Stock	Price	Discount/ Sale Price

Date: ____________________________

Theme: ____

Item Number	Item Name/Product & Description	Quantity in Stock	Price	Discount/ Sale Price

Date: ____________________________

Theme: ____

Item Number	Item Name/Product & Description	Quantity in Stock	Price	Discount/ Sale Price

Date: ______________________

Theme: ____

Item Number	Item Name/Product & Description	Quantity in Stock	Price	Discount/ Sale Price

Date: ____________________________

Theme: ____

Item Number	Item Name/Product & Description	Quantity in Stock	Price	Discount/ Sale Price

Date: ______________________

Theme: ____

Item Number	Item Name/Product & Description	Quantity in Stock	Price	Discount/ Sale Price

Date: ______________________

Theme: ____

Item Number	Item Name/Product & Description	Quantity in Stock	Price	Discount/ Sale Price

Date: ______________________

Theme: ____

Item Number	Item Name/Product & Description	Quantity in Stock	Price	Discount/ Sale Price

Date: ______________________

Theme: ____

Item Number	Item Name/Product & Description	Quantity in Stock	Price	Discount/ Sale Price

Date: ______________________

Theme: ____

Item Number	Item Name/Product & Description	Quantity in Stock	Price	Discount/ Sale Price

Date: ______________________

Theme: ____

Item Number	Item Name/Product & Description	Quantity in Stock	Price	Discount/ Sale Price

Date: ______________________

Theme: ____

Item Number	Item Name/Product & Description	Quantity in Stock	Price	Discount/ Sale Price

Date: ____________________

Theme: ____

Item Number	Item Name/Product & Description	Quantity in Stock	Price	Discount/ Sale Price

Date: ______________________

Theme: ____

Item Number	Item Name/Product & Description	Quantity in Stock	Price	Discount/ Sale Price

Date: ____________________________

Theme: ____

Item Number	Item Name/Product & Description	Quantity in Stock	Price	Discount/ Sale Price

Date: ______________________

Theme: ____

Item Number	Item Name/Product & Description	Quantity in Stock	Price	Discount/ Sale Price

Date: ______________________

Theme: ____

Item Number	Item Name/Product & Description	Quantity in Stock	Price	Discount/ Sale Price

Date: ______________________

Theme: ____

Item Number	Item Name/Product & Description	Quantity in Stock	Price	Discount/ Sale Price

Date: ____________________

Theme: ______________________________________

Item Number	Item Name/Product & Description	Quantity in Stock	Price	Discount/ Sale Price

Date: ______________________

Theme: ____

Item Number	Item Name/Product & Description	Quantity in Stock	Price	Discount/ Sale Price

Date: ______________________

Theme: ____

Item Number	Item Name/Product & Description	Quantity in Stock	Price	Discount/ Sale Price

Date: ______________________

Theme: ____

Item Number	Item Name/Product & Description	Quantity in Stock	Price	Discount/ Sale Price

Date: ______________________

Theme: ____

Item Number	Item Name/Product & Description	Quantity in Stock	Price	Discount/ Sale Price

Date: ______________________

Theme: ____

Item Number	Item Name/Product & Description	Quantity in Stock	Price	Discount/ Sale Price

Date: ____________________________

Theme: ____

Item Number	Item Name/Product & Description	Quantity in Stock	Price	Discount/ Sale Price

Date: ______________________

Theme: ____

Item Number	Item Name/Product & Description	Quantity in Stock	Price	Discount/ Sale Price

Date: ______________________

Theme: ______________________________________

Item Number	Item Name/Product & Description	Quantity in Stock	Price	Discount/ Sale Price

Date: ____________________________

Theme: ____

Item Number	Item Name/Product & Description	Quantity in Stock	Price	Discount/ Sale Price

Date: ______________________

Theme: ____

Item Number	Item Name/Product & Description	Quantity in Stock	Price	Discount/ Sale Price

Date: ______________________

Theme: ____

Item Number	Item Name/Product & Description	Quantity in Stock	Price	Discount/ Sale Price

Date: ______________________

Theme: ____

Item Number	Item Name/Product & Description	Quantity in Stock	Price	Discount/ Sale Price

Date: ____________________

Theme: ____

Item Number	Item Name/Product & Description	Quantity in Stock	Price	Discount/ Sale Price

Date: ____________________________

Theme: ____

Item Number	Item Name/Product & Description	Quantity in Stock	Price	Discount/ Sale Price

Date: ______________________

Theme: ____

Item Number	Item Name/Product & Description	Quantity in Stock	Price	Discount/ Sale Price

Date: ______________________

Theme: ____

Item Number	Item Name/Product & Description	Quantity in Stock	Price	Discount/ Sale Price

Date: ____________________

Theme: ____

Item Number	Item Name/Product & Description	Quantity in Stock	Price	Discount/ Sale Price

Date: ______________________

Theme: ____

Item Number	Item Name/Product & Description	Quantity in Stock	Price	Discount/ Sale Price

Date: ______________________

Theme: ____

Item Number	Item Name/Product & Description	Quantity in Stock	Price	Discount/ Sale Price

Date: ______________________

Theme: ____

Item Number	Item Name/Product & Description	Quantity in Stock	Price	Discount/ Sale Price

Date: ____________________________

Theme: ____

Item Number	Item Name/Product & Description	Quantity in Stock	Price	Discount/ Sale Price

Date: ______________________

Theme: ____

Item Number	Item Name/Product & Description	Quantity in Stock	Price	Discount/ Sale Price

Date: ______________________________

Theme: ____

Item Number	Item Name/Product & Description	Quantity in Stock	Price	Discount/ Sale Price

Date: ____________________

Theme: ____

Item Number	Item Name/Product & Description	Quantity in Stock	Price	Discount/ Sale Price

Date: ____________________________

Theme: ____

Item Number	Item Name/Product & Description	Quantity in Stock	Price	Discount/ Sale Price

Date: ____________________

Theme: ____

Item Number	Item Name/Product & Description	Quantity in Stock	Price	Discount/ Sale Price

Date: ____________________

Theme: ____

Item Number	Item Name/Product & Description	Quantity in Stock	Price	Discount/ Sale Price

Date: ____________________

Theme: ____

Item Number	Item Name/Product & Description	Quantity in Stock	Price	Discount/ Sale Price

Date: ______________________

Theme: ____

Item Number	Item Name/Product & Description	Quantity in Stock	Price	Discount/ Sale Price

Date: ______________________

Theme: ____

Item Number	Item Name/Product & Description	Quantity in Stock	Price	Discount/ Sale Price

Date: ______________________

Theme: ____

Item Number	Item Name/Product & Description	Quantity in Stock	Price	Discount/ Sale Price

Date: ____________________

Theme: ____

Item Number	Item Name/Product & Description	Quantity in Stock	Price	Discount/ Sale Price

Date: ______________________

Theme: ____

Item Number	Item Name/Product & Description	Quantity in Stock	Price	Discount/ Sale Price

Date: ______________________

Theme: ____

Item Number	Item Name/Product & Description	Quantity in Stock	Price	Discount/ Sale Price

Date: ______________________

Theme: ____

Item Number	Item Name/Product & Description	Quantity in Stock	Price	Discount/ Sale Price

Date: ______________________

Theme: ____

Item Number	Item Name/Product & Description	Quantity in Stock	Price	Discount/ Sale Price

Date: ______________________

Theme: ____

Item Number	Item Name/Product & Description	Quantity in Stock	Price	Discount/ Sale Price

Date: ______________________

Theme: ____

Item Number	Item Name/Product & Description	Quantity in Stock	Price	Discount/ Sale Price

Date: ____________________________

Theme: ____

Item Number	Item Name/Product & Description	Quantity in Stock	Price	Discount/ Sale Price

Date: ______________________

Theme: ____

Item Number	Item Name/Product & Description	Quantity in Stock	Price	Discount/ Sale Price

Date: ______________________

Theme: ____

Item Number	Item Name/Product & Description	Quantity in Stock	Price	Discount/ Sale Price

Date: ____________________

Theme: ____

Item Number	Item Name/Product & Description	Quantity in Stock	Price	Discount/ Sale Price

Date: ______________________

Theme: ____

Item Number	Item Name/Product & Description	Quantity in Stock	Price	Discount/ Sale Price

Date: ______________________

Theme: ____

Item Number	Item Name/Product & Description	Quantity in Stock	Price	Discount/ Sale Price

Date: ____________________

Theme: ____

Item Number	Item Name/Product & Description	Quantity in Stock	Price	Discount/ Sale Price

Date: ______________________________

Theme: ____

Item Number	Item Name/Product & Description	Quantity in Stock	Price	Discount/ Sale Price

Date: ______________________

Theme: ______________________________________

Item Number	Item Name/Product & Description	Quantity in Stock	Price	Discount/ Sale Price

Date: ______________________

Theme: ____

Item Number	Item Name/Product & Description	Quantity in Stock	Price	Discount/ Sale Price

Date: ______________________

Theme: ____

Item Number	Item Name/Product & Description	Quantity in Stock	Price	Discount/ Sale Price

Date: ____________________________

Theme: ____

Item Number	Item Name/Product & Description	Quantity in Stock	Price	Discount/ Sale Price

Date: ______________________________

Theme: ____

Item Number	Item Name/Product & Description	Quantity in Stock	Price	Discount/ Sale Price

Date: ______________________

Theme: ____

Item Number	Item Name/Product & Description	Quantity in Stock	Price	Discount/ Sale Price

Date: ______________________

Theme: ____

Item Number	Item Name/Product & Description	Quantity in Stock	Price	Discount/ Sale Price

Date: ______________________

Theme: ____

Item Number	Item Name/Product & Description	Quantity in Stock	Price	Discount/ Sale Price

Date: ______________________________

Theme: ____

Item Number	Item Name/Product & Description	Quantity in Stock	Price	Discount/ Sale Price

Date: ______________________

Theme: ____

Item Number	Item Name/Product & Description	Quantity in Stock	Price	Discount/ Sale Price

Date: ______________________

Theme: ____

Item Number	Item Name/Product & Description	Quantity in Stock	Price	Discount/ Sale Price

Date: ____________________

Theme: ____

Item Number	Item Name/Product & Description	Quantity in Stock	Price	Discount/ Sale Price

Date: ____________________________

Theme: ____

Item Number	Item Name/Product & Description	Quantity in Stock	Price	Discount/ Sale Price

Date: ______________________

Theme: ____

Item Number	Item Name/Product & Description	Quantity in Stock	Price	Discount/ Sale Price

Notes

www.ingramcontent.com/pod-product-compliance
Lightning Source LLC
Chambersburg PA
CBHW081436220526
45466CB00008B/2410
* 9 7 8 1 6 5 3 7 3 2 4 6 3 *